VERSES OF EMPOWERMENT AND INSPIRATION

DR. ESHA JAIN

DEDICATION

To Lord Krishna

My Father & my daughter Dhani

Contents

Foreword

By Dr. Deepak Jain

In the quiet chambers of a poet's heart, where words hold the power to awaken and inspire, we find ourselves on the threshold of a remarkable journey through the poetic universe crafted by Dr. Esha Jain. Within the pages of this poetry book, we embark on an odyssey through the myriad facets of the female experience, a symphony of voices that resonate with empowerment, resilience, and unwavering hope.

The table of contents before you; serves as a map, guiding us through the rich tapestry of verses that make up this collection. Each poem is a testament to the strength, wisdom, and boundless potential inherent in girls and women. Through Dr. Esha Jain's artful words, we are invited to explore the intricacies of a world where girls shatter the chains that have bound them, and women rise as guardians of their own destinies.

The journey begins with "Shattering Chains: Empowering Girls with Freedom," a clarion call for liberation and self-determination. From there, we delve into the realm of legal wisdom in "Empowering Girls Through Legal Wisdom," shedding light on the importance of knowledge and justice in the pursuit of gender equality.

As we progress through these verses, we encounter poignant themes such as the end of dowry in "Breaking Chains: The End of Dowry," financial independence in "Golden Wings: Girls Soar with Financial Independence," and the profound promise of unborn daughters in "Daughters Unborn: A Precious Promise."

We witness the delicate bloom of a daughter's hope in "The Unseen Blossom," the graceful dance of ambition and love in "Trailblazing Mothers: Balancing Love and Ambition," and the quiet heroism of homemakers in "Homemakers' Hearts: Love's Quiet Heroes."

"Sisterly Bonds: A Treasured Support" and "Daughter's Love: A Priceless Jewel" celebrate the bonds of sisterhood and parental love, while "Strength in Solitude: The Single Mother's Song" pays tribute to the resilience of single mothers.

With unwavering resolve, Dr. Esha Jain addresses the issues of violence and harassment in "Breaking the Chains: Empowering Girls Against Violence," offering a healing touch in "Healing the Shadows" and celebrating resilience in "Resilience Rising."

The poetess also turns her gaze toward the education of girls in Indian villages in "Bridging Dreams," and the shared responsibilities and chore of hearts in "Shared Responsibilities: The Chore of Hearts."

Throughout this journey, we encounter the guardians of innocence in "Guardians of Innocence: Protecting Our Daughters," the empowered warriors in "Girls Learning Self-Defense," and the champions against eve-teasing in "Break the Silence: Standing Strong Against Eve-Teasing."

Dr. Esha Jain paints a vivid portrait of the significance of women in teaching in "Shaping

Minds, Lighting Futures: Women in Teaching," and unveils the intriguing tales of notorious daughters in "The Notorious Daughter's Tale."

The collection continues to unfold, weaving a tapestry of grace in "A Tapestry of Grace: Celebrating Girls' Attributes," and ushering us into the realm of emotional freedom in "Unchained Hearts: Embracing Emotional Freedom."

As we approach the final poems, we are reminded of the importance of rights and protection in "Guardians of Rights: Celebrating Girls' Rights," and the significance of understanding boundaries in "Safe and Sound: Understanding Good and Bad Touch."

The poetic journey culminates with "Warriors of Grace," a heartfelt tribute to the resilient spirit that defines girls and women, transcending adversity and emerging as champions in their own right.

In these verses, Dr. Esha Jain has skillfully woven a tapestry of empowerment, celebrating the multifaceted strength of girls and women.

With each poem, she invites us to explore the depths of the female experience, illuminating the path toward a more equitable and just world.

I am honored to join Dr. Esha Jain on this extraordinary journey, as she invites me to walk alongside her through the labyrinth of emotions, dreams, and triumphs that define the lives of girls and women. May this collection serve as a testament to their resilience, their dreams, and their enduring spirit.

Let us begin this poetic odyssey, and may these verses forever echo in the hearts of those who read them, igniting a spark of inspiration and empowerment that will illuminate our path forward.

With Blessings

Dr. Deepak Jain
Chief Executive Officer
Nirmal Integrated Consultancy Private Limited

Eminent Endorsement: A Glowing Tribute by Dr. Binay Kumar Panjiyar

It is with profound delight that I offer my Foreword to the remarkable literary work titled 'Versus of Empowerment and Inspiration,' an anthology of socially resonant poems crafted by the distinguished wordsmith, Dr. Esha Jain, an English Poet who hails from the dynamic realm of Management.

The verses contained within this book are a tangible embodiment of emotions translated into thoughts and eloquently transcribed onto paper. I consider it a distinct honor to have had the privilege of a close association with Dr. Esha for more than a decade now. Dr. Esha Jain, whom I take immense pride in acknowledging, is not only a dear friend but also a valued well-wisher and mentor to our academic institutions.

Her dedicated contributions to the fields of management and research are widely recognized across the nation.

In 'Versus of Empowerment and Inspiration,' Dr. Esha's collection of English poems pulsates with a divine fervor that unquestionably establishes her as a distinguished English poet.

This book transcends the boundaries of education; it engenders transformative moments. The prose-poetic compositions curated within this anthology grapple with themes of love, honor, and the enduring questions that surround the essence of womanhood.

The author courageously unveils stark truths that demand our attention. Thanks to her unwavering dedication, she has made this significant body of work accessible to the masses. To put it plainly, this is an exceptional book that imparts profound insights and knowledge.

I am overwhelmed with joy that this book has come to fruition as a published work. My fervent prayer is that Dr. Esha continues to be blessed with good health and a long life, allowing her to persist in her invaluable service

to the nation as an esteemed academician,
researcher, poet, and writer of exceptional
prowess.

With Blessings

Dr. Binay Kumar Panjiyar
Associate Professor
School of Business Studies
MATS University, Raipur, Chhattisgarh

Preface

From the Poetess's Pen……

Greetings,

In the quiet spaces between words, where emotions find their voice, we discover the power of poetry. "Verses of Empowerment and Inspiration" is a collection that weaves together strength, resilience, and hope threads. These poems celebrate the spirit of girls and women, delving into topics that range from education and empowerment to courage and freedom.

In the midst of life's challenges, these verses stand as a testament to the indomitable spirit of girls, women, and the people who support them. Through these words, we aim to inspire and uplift, shed light on important issues, and celebrate the beauty of love, strength, and courage.

Each poem is a brushstroke on the canvas of empowerment, each title a beacon of inspiration. We invite you to explore the pages of this collection, where you'll find poetry as a source of reflection, motivation, and a reminder that, together, we can create a world where every girl and woman shines brightly.

May these verses resonate with your heart and ignite the flames of empowerment within you. With each line, may you find solace, strength, and inspiration to make a positive difference in the world. Thank you for joining us on this journey of empowerment through the power of poetry.

With boundless hope,
Dr. Esha Jain

Acknowledgements

Whispers of Gratitude

In the tapestry of life's verses, there are many threads of gratitude to weave. I am immensely thankful to the universe for the gift of inspiration. To Lord Krishna, my father, and my whole world - my daughter Dhani whose unwavering support and love have been my wellspring of creativity, I offer my deepest appreciation. To my friends and fellow poets, thank you for being my poetic companions on this journey. To all the readers who seek empowerment and inspiration in these verses, I dedicate this collection with heartfelt gratitude. Your presence in my poetic world is the ultimate honor.

~ Dr. Esha Jain

Prologue

"Verses of Empowerment and Inspiration" is a compelling collection of poems celebrating girls' and women's resilience, strength, and dreams. Through the power of poetry, this book delves into topics such as education, self-defense, emotional freedom, and the rights of girls. It sheds light on important issues while offering words of encouragement and motivation.

These verses stand as a testament to the indomitable spirit of girls and women, painting a vivid picture of their journey towards empowerment. The collection aims to inspire readers, urging them to reflect on the beauty of love, strength, and courage.

In a world filled with challenges, "Verses of Empowerment and Inspiration" serves as a source of reflection and a reminder that we can create a more inclusive and empowered world for every girl and woman. This book is an invitation to explore the transformative power of poetry and to embrace the idea that positive change begins with inspiration.

Whether you seek motivation or simply a moment of solace, these poems offer a meaningful and uplifting reading experience. Join us on a journey of empowerment through the beauty of words and let these verses ignite the flames of inspiration within you.

1. Shattering Chains: Empowering Girls with Freedom

Independence, a girl's rightful claim,
A journey of freedom, her life's aim.

With dreams in her heart, she'll take flight,
Independence, her guiding light so bright.

Breaking societal norms, she'll emerge strong,
Her voice, a melody, her spirit, a song.

From dependence to self-belief, she'll rise,
To the skies of freedom, where her spirit flies.

Education and courage, her tools in hand,
Independence, a gift, a promised land.

In a world of possibilities, she'll chart her way,
With each step she takes, a brighter day.

No longer bound, no longer confined,
Independence, a treasure, in her heart enshrined.

So let us nurture this flame within,
Independence for girls, a vital win.

For when they stand free, the world will see,
The power and potential of girls, let it be.

In the tapestry of life, let their threads be spun,
Independence for girls, until it's won.

2. Empowering Girls Through Legal Wisdom

In the realm of justice, girls must find their way,
Legal education, a guiding light to obey.

To grasp society's rules, to know right from wrong,
Empowering girls, through knowledge, strong.

Defend their rights, and justice uphold,
Legal education, a treasure of gold.

With expertise in law, they'll stand tall,
Breaking down barriers, scaling every wall.

In a world of complexities, where fairness is key,
Legal education, their tool to set them free.

For in their hands, they'll hold the might,
To champion justice, to make things right.

So, let's empower girls with legal insight,
A world where they thrive, shining so bright.

In the pursuit of justice, let them unfurl,
Their potential and strength as legal pearls.

3. Breaking Chains: The End of Dowry

In the shadows of tradition, a practice so old,
Dowry's burden on shoulders, heavy and cold.

But a new dawn is rising, a change in the air,
The call to abolish this system, we all share.

No longer a price tag, for a daughter's hand,
Her worth defined not by the dowry's demand.

For love and respect should be the foundation,
Not material wealth, not an obligation.

Families unite, raising voices high,
To end this injustice, to let love fly.

Empower the girls, let them stand tall,
No longer victims, but leaders for all.

With education and dreams, they'll break free,
From the chains of dowry, they'll finally see.

A world where love reigns, not money's decree,
The abolition of dowry, our victory decree.

Let's celebrate this change, this new start,
A society where love conquers every heart.

4. Golden Wings: Girls Soar with Financial Independence

In a world of dreams and boundless skies,
Financial independence, a precious prize.

Girls spread their wings, they aim to fly,
No longer dependent, reaching for the sky.

Education their beacon, knowledge their might,
They conquer the darkness, embrace the light.

With skills and ambition, they chart their own course,
Financial independence, their powerful force.

No more reliance, no more compromise,
They seize their future, they'll claim the prize.

Empowered and strong, they'll stand side by side,
With financial independence, their joy multiplied.

Breaking through barriers, they shatter the ceiling,
Their dreams and aspirations, there's no concealing.

In a world of opportunity, they'll find their way,
With financial independence, they'll seize the day.

So, let's celebrate their strength and resilience,
Financial independence, a path of brilliance.

For when girls are free to chase their dreams,
The world becomes brighter, or so it seems.

5. Daughters Unborn: A Precious Promise

In the secret chambers of the womb's embrace,
Lies a tiny being, a future's trace.

A female foetus, a world yet unknown,
A promise of beauty, yet to be shown.

Innocence wrapped in a fragile form,
A daughter's existence, a calm before the storm.

Yet, in some hearts, a shadow may loom,
As prejudices and fears attempt to consume.

But hold dear the hope, let love persist,
For a daughter's presence, we must insist.

She's a future leader, a beacon of grace,
A symbol of strength in this vast human race.

Her laughter, her dreams, her potential untold,
Are treasures within her, more precious than gold.

Let us protect, nurture, and cherish her fate,
For daughters unborn, it's never too late.

In their existence, we find our true worth,
A promise of love, a testament to our Earth.

So let the world know, in word and in deed,
Daughters are precious, there's no greater need.

For in the hearts of daughters, we find,
A reflection of love, forever intertwined.

6. The Unseen Blossom: A Daughter's Hope

In the hidden chambers of life's grand design,
A daughter waits, in the shadows confined.

A female foetus, a treasure yet concealed,
A world of promise, yet to be revealed.

Amidst the silence of her mother's core,
A seed of potential, a future to explore.

Innocence veiled by the womb's tender hold,
A story of strength, waiting to be told.

But sometimes, society casts a dark shade,
Discrimination and bias, in the choices made.

Yet, let us not forget the beauty within,
The power of daughters, where victories begin.

For she's a dreamer, a force to be reckoned,
Her worth, in the world, is yet to be beckoned.

With every heartbeat, her spirit does swell,
A testament to love, her story to tell.

Her laughter, her tears, her dreams to unfold,
Are treasures within her, more precious than gold.

Let's protect, nurture, and let her be free,
For daughters are the heartbeats of destiny.

In her existence, we find endless grace,
A glimpse of tomorrow, a future's embrace.

So, celebrate her presence, loud and clear,
For daughters are a promise, a reason to cheer.

The unseen blossom, with potential so vast,
A daughter's hope, in the world's heart, shall last.

7. Trailblazing Mothers: Balancing Love and Ambition

In the world of dreams and aspirations high,
Career-oriented mothers reach for the sky.

Balancing love and ambition with grace,
They carve their path in life's bustling race.

With briefcases and strollers, they stride,
With dreams in their hearts, nowhere to hide.

Their children's future, a beacon so bright,
They chase their goals with all their might.

In the boardroom or at the kitchen table,
They juggle responsibilities, they're able.

Career-oriented mothers, bold and wise,
Breaking barriers beneath the endless skies.

Their little ones watch, in admiration,
Learning the art of determination.

For these mothers, a source of inspiration,
Balancing love and their vocation.

With love, they nurture, with dreams they inspire,
Their children's hearts, they set on fire.

Career-oriented mothers, strong and true,
The world is a better place because of you.

So, here's to mothers, who lead the way,
Paving the road for a brighter day.

Balancing love and ambition's fire,
Career-oriented mothers, you inspire.

8. Homemakers' Hearts: Love's Quiet Heroes

In the heart of the home, their love takes its place,
Housewife mothers, with smiles on their face.

Their days are filled with tasks, both big and small,
Creating a haven, where love touches all.

With aprons tied and hands so busy,
They make a house a home, oh so cozy.

From breakfast to bedtime, their care never ends,
Housewife mothers, on them, we depend.

They mend torn clothes and mend wounded hearts,
Their love, like a tapestry, weaves life's parts.

From cleaning and cooking to comforting too,
Housewife mothers, we're grateful to you.

They teach us life's lessons, values, and grace,
Their wisdom and love in every embrace.

In laughter and tears, they stand by our side,
Housewife mothers, in them, we confide.

Their strength lies in patience, resilience their guide,
Housewife mothers, with hearts open wide.

Their sacrifices made with love, not a fuss,
For in the warmth of their love, we find our trust.

So, here's to homemakers, in love they immerse,
Their value and worth, let's not disperse.

Housewife mothers, love's quiet heroes, they stand,
In the heart of the home, guiding hand in hand.

9. Sisterly Bonds: A Treasured Support

In the tapestry of life, a bond so sweet,
Sisterly affection, a love complete.

Through thick and thin, in sunshine or rain,
A sister's support, an unbreakable chain.

With shared secrets and dreams so vast,
In each other's company, time flies so fast.

In laughter and tears, we stand side by side,
A sister's love, a lifelong guide.

When the world seems cold, and troubles arise,
A sister's presence, a comforting surprise.

With a hug and a smile, she eases the load,
A sister's love, an unspoken code.

Through the ups and downs, the highs and lows,
A sister's affection, like a warm wind that blows.

She lifts you up when you're feeling low,
A sister's support, like a steady, gentle flow.

In her company, you find solace and cheer,
A sister's love, so precious and dear.

With understanding eyes and a listening ear,
A sister's bond, forever sincere.

So, cherish this gift, this love so true,
A sister's affection, always there for you.

Through life's journey, come what may,
Sisterly support, forever to stay.

10. Daughter's Love: A Priceless Jewel

In the heart of a daughter, a love so pure,
A bond that's timeless, forever secure.

Her laughter, her tears, her smiles that gleam,
A daughter's love, like a radiant dream.

From the first breath she took, a father's delight,
A mother's joy, in the day and the night.

In her tiny hands, a world to behold,
A daughter's love, more precious than gold.

Through childhood's trials and teenage strife,
A daughter's love, the essence of life.

In her hugs and her words, the warmth of the sun,
A daughter's love, second to none.

As she grows, her love only grows stronger,
A love that will last, a love that's no longer.

Bound by the years, but by love's sweet decree,
A daughter's love, pure and free.

In her dreams and her hopes, her heart's sweet song,
A daughter's love, it's where we all belong.

A treasure, a blessing, beyond all measure,
A daughter's love, a love to treasure forever.

11. Strength in Solitude: The Single Mother's Song

In the realm of solitude, she stands tall,
A single mother, giving her all.

With strength in her heart, and love in her eyes,
She faces the world, wearing no disguise.

Through the stormy nights and the sunlit days,
She weaves a future in countless ways.

With grace and courage, she paves her own road,
A single mother, carrying her load.

In the quiet moments, when the world is asleep,
She dreams of a promise, a commitment so deep.

Her love knows no bounds, her spirit so high,
A single mother, reaching for the sky.

With little hands to hold and dreams to inspire,
She never falters, she never tires.

In her love's embrace, her children find home,
A single mother, they'll never be alone.

Through life's twists and turns, she remains strong,
A single mother, where love belongs.

In her embrace, there's comfort and care,
A single mother, always willing to share.

So, let's celebrate her, with respect and grace,
A single mother's journey, in life's embrace.

In her strength and love, she stands so proud,
A single mother's song, sung strong and loud.

12. The Only Girl: A Precious Pearl

In a world of siblings, she stands alone,
The only girl, in a family of her own.

With eyes that sparkle and dreams so wild,
She's the family's treasure, their only girl child.

In her laughter and tears, she lights up their days,
With her love and her charm, in countless ways.

She's the center of attention, the heart's delight,
The only girl, shining ever so bright.

With grace and strength, she charts her way,
In a world where she'll conquer, come what may.

Her parents' pride, their love's sweet pearl,
The only girl, in the family's swirl.

She's a sister, a daughter, and a friend so dear,
Her presence brings joy, dispelling every fear.

In her love's embrace, they find their peace,
The only girl, their love will never cease.

So, celebrate her presence, in every way,
The only girl, brightening each and every day.

In her uniqueness, she's a treasure to hold,
A precious pearl, more valuable than gold.

13. Daughter-In-Law: A Bond So Dear

In the tapestry of life, a new thread's sewn,
A daughter-in-law, a love warmly known.

With grace in her step, and a heart so pure,
She joins the family, a love to endure.

A bridge between families, cultures entwined,
Her love and kindness, a treasure we find.

In her laughter and tears, her strength so clear,
A daughter-in-law, we hold her near.

She brings joy and warmth to each family meal,
Her love, like a secret, a bond she'll seal.

With respect and care, her role she'll embrace,
A daughter-in-law, with love's gentle grace.

In the hearts of her in-laws, she finds her place,
A daughter-in-law, with a smiling face.

In her presence, our hearts find cheer,
A bond that's cherished, year after year.

So, let's celebrate this bond so true,
A daughter-in-law, a gift that's due.

In her, we find a friend so dear,
A relationship to hold, to honor, to revere.

14. Sisters-In-Law: Hearts Aflame

Sisters-in-law, with hearts so kind,
A unique bond, a precious find.

United by marriage, fate's design,
In each other's lives, a bright sunshine.

Nanad's wisdom, a guiding light,
Bhabhi's warmth, a love so right.

Together they laugh, they share, they care,
A bond so special, beyond compare.

In moments of joy and times of strife,
They stand together in the dance of life.

With secrets whispered and stories untold,
A friendship that's priceless, a love to behold.

Through the twists and turns, they remain true,
A bond between sisters, forever in view.

In each other's hearts, they find their place,
Sisters-in-law, an embrace of grace.

So, let's celebrate this unique connection,
A bond of love, beyond mere reflection.

In their relationship, we see no divide,
Sisters-in-law, side by side, they ride.

15. Breaking the Chains: Empowering Girls Against Violence

In the shadows of fear, they silently bear,
Physical violence, a burden unfair.

But the time has come to make a stand,
Empowering girls, hand in hand.

With courage in their hearts, they'll rise above,
The cycle of violence, the push and the shove.

No more the victims, their strength will shine,
Empowering girls, it's their time to define.

To break the chains, to reclaim their voice,
In unity and love, they'll make the choice.

To end the torment, to seek the light,
Empowering girls, they'll win the fight.

In their hearts, they hold the key,
To a world where violence should never be.

With love and support, they'll heal the scar,
Empowering girls, no matter how far.

So, let's stand together, hand in hand,
Empowering girls, to take a stand.

To end the violence, to break the chain,
In a world of love, let freedom reign.

16. Healing the Shadows

In the darkest corners, where shadows loom,
A painful silence, a victim's room.

A crime so vile, that shatters the soul,
The word 'rape' leaves an endless toll.

But in the midst of pain, there's strength within,
A survivor's spirit, a chance to begin.

To heal the wounds, to find the light,
In the battle for justice, they'll stand and fight.

No more hiding, no more shame,
Speaking their truth, they'll reclaim their name.

In unity and love, they'll find their way,
Together they'll rise, come what may.

For the world must change, must heed the call,
To prevent this darkness, once and for all.

To educate, to support, to erase the stain,
In the fight against rape, we'll break the chain.

Let us stand with survivors, in solidarity,
In the face of violence, with empathy.

For healing takes time, but they'll find their grace,
In the journey towards justice, in this sacred space.

17. Resilience Rising

In the depths of despair, they found their way,
Acid survivors, facing a brand-new day.

With courage and strength, they rise above,
Their scars tell stories of resilience and love.

Though the world turned cruel, and fate unkind,
They embrace their beauty, their spirits unwind.

In the mirror, they see strength in their gaze,
Acid survivors, rewriting life's craze.

Each scar is a badge of their enduring grace,
A testament to courage in the toughest space.

In the face of adversity, they stand tall,
Acid survivors, they conquer it all.

Through pain and tears, they bloom like a flower,
Their inner strength, an incredible power.

To rebuild their lives, their dreams they chase,

Acid survivors, in love's warm embrace.

In unity, let's support their brave ascent,
Help them heal, their confidence reinvent.

For in their stories, there's a truth to be seen,
Acid survivors, champions so serene.

In the journey to recovery, they find their way,
Acid survivors, beacons of hope today.

Resilience rising, their spirits ignite,
Shining as stars in the darkest night.

18. Bridging Dreams: Girls' Education in Indian Villages

In the heart of rural India's vast expanse,
Lies the promise of girls, a chance to advance.

Amidst fields of green and rivers that flow,
A desire for education, a dream's soft glow.

In the humble village schools, they take their place,
With bright eyes, they strive, they run the race.

For knowledge is the key to break the chains,
Girls' education, where opportunity gains.

With uniforms crisp and books in hand,
They embrace learning, like grains of sand.

In the classroom's embrace, they find their voice,
Girls' education, a powerful choice.

Though obstacles loom, like mountains so high,
They're determined to reach for the sky.

For their dreams are boundless, their spirits so free,
Girls' education, a gateway to be.

In the warmth of the teacher's guiding care,
They discover a world, so rich and fair.

With every lesson, they spread their wings wide,
Girls' education, a transformative tide.

In Indian villages, where dreams take flight,
Girls' education, a beacon of light.

A brighter future, they'll surely sow,
With knowledge and wisdom, they'll continue to grow.

So, let's celebrate their journey, their quest,
Girls' education, in India's vibrant chest.

For in their learning, the nation finds its grace,
Bridging dreams and futures, in this sacred space.

19. Shared Responsibilities: The Chore of Hearts

In the heart of a home, where love resides,
Responsibilities are shared, like ocean tides.

From sweeping the floors to cooking with grace,
Household chores are a journey we all embrace.

A chore is not a burden, but a duty of hearts,
In the tapestry of life, it's a vital part.

From making a bed to tending the yard,
Each task brings us close, our bond not marred.

In the kitchen's warm embrace, we create,
Delicious meals, memories that resonate.

From washing the dishes to setting the table,
Household chores, like a family fable.

Laundry days, a rhythm of life's song,
Folding clothes together, where we all belong.

From dusting the shelves to mopping the floors,
In shared responsibilities, love always pours.

So, let's not see chores as mundane or bleak,
But a chance to connect, a bond to speak.

In the chore of hearts, our love shines bright,
Together we'll make our home a warm delight.

Responsibilities, a shared journey we tread,
With love and laughter, in every thread.

In the tapestry of life, our connection soars,
With shared responsibilities, our love restores.

20. Guardians of Innocence: Protecting Our Daughters

In a world where shadows sometimes loom,
We stand as protectors, in every room.

With hearts ablaze and love so deep,
We guard our daughters as they sleep.

Their innocence, a fragile, precious thing,
In our embrace, they find their wings.

To shield them from harm, our solemn vow,
We'll protect them then, we're protecting now.

From the darkest corners, we'll keep them away,
In the light of love, they'll safely stay.

We'll teach them strength, we'll teach them grace,
Empowering them to find their place.

In a world that sometimes seems unkind,
We'll be their shelter, their peace of mind.

For daughters are treasures, a precious pearl,
In their protection, our love will unfurl.

With every heartbeat, we'll guard and guide,
Through life's challenges, we'll be by their side.

Our daughters' safety, our utmost care,
In our love's embrace, they'll find solace there.

So let us stand strong, our duty clear,
To protect our daughters, we'll hold them near.

With love as our armor, they'll always thrive,
In our protective embrace, they'll truly come alive.

21. Empowered Warriors: Girls Learning Self-Defense

In a world where strength knows no gender,
Girls learn to defend, they're fierce contenders.

With courage and grit, they stand tall and strong,
Self-defense, their shield against all wrong.

They master the moves, each technique they learn,
In self-defense classes, their skills they discern.

With focus and discipline, they train each day,
Empowered warriors, they're here to stay.

From punches to kicks, and holds to blocks,
They conquer their fears, like mighty rocks.

In self-defense, they find their voice,
Empowered girls, they rise, they rejoice.

No longer afraid, no longer confined,
They break through barriers, they redefine.

In their newfound strength, they find their grace,
Empowered warriors, in life's embrace.

In self-defense, they discover their might,
They'll stand up for justice, they'll shine so bright.

With confidence and skill, they'll pave the way,
Empowered girls, a force to sway.

So, let's celebrate their journey, their might,
Girls learning self-defense, in the day and night.

In their empowerment, a future we see,
A world where girls walk tall, wild and free.

22. Break the Silence: Standing Strong Against Eve-Teasing

In the streets and lanes, where shadows creep,
A menace called eve-teasing; a secret so deep.

But we'll break the silence, we'll stand up tall,
Against this injustice, we'll give our all.

For every girl deserves respect and grace,
To walk the streets, to claim her space.

Eve-teasing, an act of cowardice and shame,
We'll challenge this culture; we'll change the game.

With voices united, we'll rise above,
In the name of justice, in the name of love.

No longer silent, no longer afraid,
We'll empower the girls, a future remade.

In the fight against eve-teasing, we'll unite,
To make our streets safe, day and night.

With courage and strength, we'll pave the way,
For a world where respect will forever stay.

So, let's raise our voices, let's take a stand,
For a world where girls can walk hand in hand.

Eve-teasing, we'll conquer and defy,
In the face of courage, it will wither and die.

23. Protecting Our Innocence

In the innocence of youth, we all must strive,
To keep our children safe and alive.

For child molestation is a dark abyss,
We must protect our children, we can't dismiss.

Their trust is sacred, their hearts so pure,
In their laughter and smiles, we must ensure.

No harm will come, no pain they'll endure,
Child molestation, we must secure.

Their dreams are fragile, their spirits so free,
In their world of wonder, we must decree.

That predators and darkness will never be,
Allowed to hurt them, we must agree.

With love and vigilance, we'll stand as one,
To protect our daughters, our daughters, and sons.

Child molestation, we'll fight and oppose,
In the name of safety, our love overflows.

Let's educate and raise awareness high,
To ensure our children can spread their wings and fly.

Child molestation, we'll banish from sight,
In the warm embrace of love and light.

24. Shaping Minds, Lighting Futures: Women in Teaching

In the classrooms of hope, where minds take flight,
Women in teaching, a guiding light.

With knowledge and patience, they lead the way,
Shaping the future, come what may.

With a heart full of wisdom and lessons to share,
They nurture young minds with love and care.

In the world of learning, they stand so tall,
Empowering each student to give their all.

Through laughter and challenges, they inspire and mold,
In the stories they tell, in the wisdom they hold.

Women in teaching, with voices so kind,
In the hearts of their students, their influence we find.

They instill not just facts but values so pure,
In the classroom of life, their lessons endure.

With dedication and passion, they shape the dreams,
Of generations to come, like flowing streams.

So, let's celebrate these educators, so wise,
Women in teaching, they touch the skies.

Guiding the future, lighting the way,
In the hearts of their students, their impact will stay.

25. The Notorious Daughter's Tale

In a world where rules often bind,
Lived a daughter with a mischievous mind.

Notorious, she was, a free-spirited heart,
In her own wild world, she chose to chart.

With a twinkle in her eye and laughter in her voice,
She made unconventional choices, her own unique choice.

Notorious, they said, with a hint of a smile,
As she danced to her tune, mile after mile.

Her spirit was fierce, her dreams were bold,
In the pages of her story, countless tales told.

Notorious, they whispered, in tones of surprise,
As she reached for the stars, up in the skies.

In a world of conformity, she stood apart,
A free-thinking rebel, with a courageous heart.

Notorious, yes, she wore it with pride,
In her notorious journey, she'd never hide.

For she was a daughter who dared to be free,
Writing her story with wild, fierce glee.

Notorious, her legend, will forever remain,
A girl who danced to her own vibrant refrain.

26. A Tapestry of Grace: Celebrating Girls' Attributes

In the canvas of life, girls paint a scene,
With attributes diverse, a rainbow's sheen.

Each one unique, a work of art,
In their essence and presence, they set hearts apart.

With strength and resilience, they weather the storm,
Facing adversity, they transform.

Attributes like courage, they wear as their shield,
In the face of challenges, they never yield.

In kindness and empathy, they extend a hand,
Spreading love and understanding across the land.

Attributes like compassion, they hold so dear,
In their hearts, they keep the world so near.

With wisdom and knowledge, they seek to explore,
Unlocking the mysteries, they hunger for more.

Attributes like curiosity, they'll always possess,
In their pursuit of truth, they're sure to impress.

In the tapestry of life, they weave their grace,
With attributes so diverse, in every place.

Girls, like stars, they brightly shine,
In their attributes, a world so divine.

So, let's celebrate these attributes, so grand,
In the world of girls, where dreams expand.

A tapestry of grace, a sight to behold,
In the hearts of girls, our stories are told.

27. Unchained Hearts: Embracing Emotional Freedom

In a world that often seeks to confine,
Girls yearn for freedom, an emotional sign.

To express their feelings, to laugh, to cry,
Emotional freedom, let their spirits fly high.

No more hiding behind societal walls,
They'll break the constraints; they'll heed the calls.

To love and to dream, to be bold and strong,
Emotional freedom, where they truly belong.

With hearts wide open and minds unbound,
They'll explore their feelings, their depths to be found.

In a world that's evolving, they'll take the lead,
Emotional freedom, it's their deepest need.

To be heard and respected, in every way,
They'll speak their truth, come what may.

In their emotional freedom, they'll find their voice,
A powerful presence, a force to rejoice.

So, let's support their journey, let them thrive,
In the realm of emotions, let them come alive.

Emotional freedom, a gift so divine,
In the hearts of girls, let it forever shine.

28. Guardians of Rights: Celebrating Girls' Rights

In the tapestry of life, a truth we must uphold,
Girls' rights are precious, more valuable than gold.

With voices strong, they'll take their stand,
For equal rights, they'll lend a helping hand.

To education and dreams, they have a rightful claim,
Girls' rights, an essential part of the game.

No longer silenced, no longer ignored,
In the fight for equality, they'll be adored.

To live without fear, to pursue their dreams,
Girls' rights, like a river, in the sunbeams.

In a world of opportunity, they'll find their way,
For girls' rights, we'll celebrate each day.

In their voices, in their dreams, they hold the key,
To a future where girls' rights are a guarantee.

For in their strength and determination, we see,
A world where equality is the decree.

So, let's stand as allies, in their courageous flight,
Guardians of rights, let's shine the light.

Girls' rights, a beacon, let them brightly shine,
In a world where equality is the ultimate sign.

29. Safe and Sound: Understanding Good and Bad Touch

In the realm of touch, where boundaries reside,
It's crucial to know the feelings inside.

Good and bad touch, we must understand,
To keep ourselves safe in this fragile land.

A good touch is warm, gentle, and kind,
A hug from a loved one, a friend you can find.

It's a pat on the back, a reassuring hold,
A touch that makes you feel cherished and bold.

But beware of the bad touch, a warning to heed,
It's invasive and hurtful, it's not what we need.

A touch that's uncomfortable, causing you pain,
Speak out, seek help, let your voice gain.

In the world we inhabit, where trust is a must,
We must teach our children, whom they can trust.

To differentiate the good from the bad,
So, they stay safe and never feel sad.

In understanding the difference, we hold the key,
To protect ourselves, to live fearlessly.

Good and bad touch, let's educate all,
To ensure a world where safety stands tall.

With knowledge and courage, we'll stand our ground,
In the realm of touch, where safety is found.

Good and bad touch, we'll teach and impart,
To keep our loved ones safe, close to our heart.

30. Warriors of Grace

In the tapestry of life, they take their place,
Girls and women, warriors with grace.

With strength in their hearts, and courage untamed,
They rise to the challenges, unashamed.

In the battles they fight, with armor unseen,
They're warriors of love, their spirits serene.

With resilience and hope, they march side by side,
Girls and women, in whom we take pride.

They conquer their fears, break through the chains,
In the face of adversity, they still remain.

With wisdom and kindness, they lead the way,
Girls and women, a shining array.

In the darkest of hours, they're beacons of light,
Guiding us forward, through the darkest night.

With love as their weapon, and justice their shield,

They fight for a world where compassion is revealed.

So, let's celebrate their strength, their valor so true,
Girls and women, the warriors we look up to.

In their journey of courage, they lead the parade,
Warriors of grace, forever unafraid.

About The Poetess

Dr. Esha Jain stands as an eminent academician with over sixteen years of remarkable expertise in finance, accounting, and entrepreneurship. Armed with a Ph.D. and UGC-NET qualifications, she is celebrated for her outstanding contributions to education and research.

Her accolades include prestigious awards such as the 'Eminent Educationist Award,' 'Asia Pacific Gold Star Award,' 'Young Woman Educator and Scholar Award,' and the esteemed 'Excellence Award.' Dr. Jain's remarkable achievements extend to being selected for the prestigious 'Rajiv Gandhi Education Excellence Award' and the 'Bharat Vidya Shiromani Award.'

As a pivotal Resource Person, she contributes significantly to Faculty Development Programs, Workshops, Conferences, Seminars, and Webinars at both national and international levels. Dr. Jain's expertise is underscored by 33 Honors and Awards, including 22 Best Research Paper Awards and the coveted Dean Committee Choice Award in renowned International Conferences.

Her engagement in academia reaches new heights as IIM Indore invited her to review 'Institutional Development Plans (IDPs)' under the World Bank-supported Madhya Pradesh Higher Education Quality Improvement Project (MPHEQIP), to be presented to the Department of Higher Education, Government of Madhya Pradesh.

Dr. Jain's commitment to impart continuous learning is evident in the training modules that she provided at the Chartered Institute of Management Accountants (CIMA), London, UK. She is also certified by the Institute of Chartered Accountants of India (ICAI) to conduct 'Investor Awareness Programmes' in various institutions and organizations.

Dr. Jain's proficiency extends across various domains, including NAAC, NBA, NIRF, ARIIA, IIC, and more, alongside her expertise in Finance and Entrepreneurship subjects.

Her prolific research contributions shine through the publication of over 100 research papers in esteemed International Journals, including Scopus, Web of Science, and UGC Care. Dr. Jain has authored four books of high repute, cementing her status as a distinguished author.

Notably, she has published sixteen patents with the Government of India, showcasing her prowess in innovation and research. Dr. Jain's academic influence transcends borders, with over 80 research papers and cases presented at numerous national and international conferences. Her role as a Session Chair, Keynote Speaker, and Panelist in Panel Discussions at various National and International Seminars and Conferences further solidifies her esteemed stature in academia.

She can be reached at dr.eshajain1985@gmail.com.